MY MOTHER WITH A BEETLE IN HER HAIR

SELIMA HILL

All rights reserved. No part of this work covered by the copyright herein may be reproduced or used in any means—graphic, electronic, or mechanical, including copying, recording, taping, or information storage and retrieval systems—without written permission of the publisher.

Printed by imprintdigital
Upton Pyne, Exeter
www.digital.imprint.co.uk

Typesetting by narrator
www.narrator.me.uk
info@narrator.me.uk
033 022 300 39

Cover design by Maisie Hill

Published by Shoestring Press
19 Devonshire Avenue, Beeston, Nottingham, NG9 1BS
(0115) 925 1827
www.shoestringpress.co.uk

First published 2020
© Copyright: Selima Hill
© Cover image: Selima Hill

The moral right of the author has been asserted.

ISBN 978-1-912524-72-3

To Dot

W FOR WATER BEETLE

The water beetle here shall teach
A sermon far beyond your reach:
He flabbergasts the Human Race
By gliding on the water's face
With ease, celerity and grace;
But if he ever stopped to think
Of how he did it, he would sink.

~Hilaire Belloc

CONTENTS

Owls	1
My Uncle the Doctor	2
My Mother's Hands	3
My Mother Wearing More than One Coat	4
The Pool Attendant at Night	5
The Man Who Looks Like a Baby	6
The Woman from the Nail Bar	7
Walnut Whips	8
Her One Desire	9
Different Kinds of Honey	10
My Mother's Daughter	11
My Mother and the Sheep	12
Looking at Each Other's Breasts in the Changing-Room	13
My Mother as a Daisy	14
Café in the Snow	15
The Man with Snow-White Skin	16
A Woman with a Bunch of Red Roses	17
Having Fun with Babies	18
An Old Man Blue with Cold	19
The Woman with the Plait	20
Rabbits	21
Friday Night at the Swimming-pool	22
The Man in Purple Swimming-Trunks	23
The Photograph of my Dog in my Duffle-Bag	24
A Very Dark Blue	25
The Silent Couple No One Really Knows	26
The Woman in the Salmon-Pink Underwear	27
Delicate Questions from the Young Doctor	28
Expensive Swimwear	29
No More Potatoes	30

OWLS

Because I had to do my homework first
and even then she only let me swim
for twenty minutes at the very most
I'd wait until my mother was asleep
and tiptoe to the lake
on my own,
barely breathing
in the cold and dark
when nothing can be heard but the owls
who've no idea how lucky they are.

MY UNCLE THE DOCTOR

On very rare occasions
my uncle
would take me to the baths
in a taxi
and afterwards,
inside the vast entrance hall,
he'd offer me an evil-looking chocolate,
it was black and tasted of black rot,
of forest floors that never see the light,
but I was much too proud
to spit it out
and anyway I had to be careful,
my uncle was a doctor
and doctors
will operate on girls who are ungrateful,
even those, like me, who could swim,
my tiny head encased in a bathing-cap
that smelled of what it smells like inside mountains
inhabited by wolverines and moles.

MY MOTHER'S HANDS

When I was a child I would duck
every time I saw the bony hands
my mother used to gaze at,
full of sorrow,
as if she wished they weren't the hands she touched me with
when—feel them—
she towelled me roughly dry.

MY MOTHER WEARING MORE THAN ONE COAT

I'm white and wrinkly
but I won't stop swimming
in spite of what my little mother told me,
although to call her *little's* not polite
but I was like that then,
so impolite,
so inconsiderate and unpredictable
and she was small
and didn't like the water
and felt the cold
even on dry land,
even in her rugs,
in several coats,
she wanted to go home
but I ignored her.

THE POOL ATTENDANT AT NIGHT

When we've all gone home
he'll lock the doors,
turn the lights out,
take off all his clothes
and slide into the pool like a newt
that thinks it's not a newt but a pool attendant.

THE MAN WHO LOOKS LIKE A BABY

He sits beside the water-cooler, smiling,
and rubs his face,
he can't see a thing,
he lets me be not only me but anyone,
here, like him, to dream,
to not be vertical,
adopting funny shapes like fried eggs.

THE WOMAN FROM THE NAIL BAR

At six o'clock she eats some cottage cheese
and then she swims
until she can't go on,
until she crushes any hopes of happiness
like snails
on the changing-room floor.

WALNUT WHIPS

When my mother died
I think I felt
not so much broken
as whole
like one of those walnuts
on cakes
or Walnut Whips
that anyway *look* whole.

HER ONE DESIRE

As I fought my way through the duckweed
that spread across the surface of a lake
the size and shape of something like a concert hall
full of chairs and pianos
made of water
and disappeared between the slimy legs
of sofas made of root
with mud cushions
inhabited by ancient-looking trout,
my mother would be waving from the bank,
her one desire
to see me wrapped up warmly.

DIFFERENT KINDS OF HONEY

While the two elaborately-wrinkled women,
should I call them women or ladies,
who look like ballerinas
or ex-ballerinas,
no, I'd better call them ballet-*dancers,*
ballet-*dancers* doesn't sound so girly,
while they stand beside the red NO JUMPING sign
and talk about different kinds of honey,
they totally ignore me,
I'm ignored,
like mashed potato sitting on the plate
of somebody I know
in her wheelchair
repeating in her little piping voice
potato and *potato* and *potato*
but actually I like to be ignored,
to think I look so normal I'm ignorable,
I'm like a sort of spy, I suppose

MY MOTHER'S DAUGHTER

Because I was a difficult child,
violent, morose and inconsolable,
endurance swimming suited me perfectly
but no, my mother called it
showing off,
she had this thing I wanted her attention.
although that was the last thing that I wanted,
every breath I took said *go away,*
every little breath,
as, rain or shine,
she sat beside the water underneath
various annoying-looking hats.

MY MOTHER AND THE SHEEP

Once I came downstairs to find a sheep
standing in the kitchen
and my mother
offering the sheep
a ginger biscuit
and looking overjoyed
to have a sheep
suddenly arrive
in her kitchen,
it used to reappear,
I remember,
and fall asleep
in my mother's lap
and keep her nice and warm
while I was swimming.

LOOKING AT EACH OTHER'S BREASTS IN THE CHANGING-ROOM

When to speak the truth was not allowed,
to be undressed,
to look,
was not allowed,
we didn't know we wouldn't mind a bit
how leathery our breasts are
or how few.

MY MOTHER AS A DAISY

As I swim serenely up and down
I strip her of the ankle-length mackintosh
she used to sit and wait in on the bank
underneath a pile of old blankets,
and dress her in a tutu
like a daisy
and offer her a corps of smaller daises
all of whom would rather die
than swim
and sometimes I imagine her on horseback—
somewhere she said girls
should never sit,
never wearing any kind of trouser
and certainly not cracking a whip—
rushing past
cracking a whip.

CAFÉ IN THE SNOW

Later I thought
I shouldn't have gone
in the first place
a snowy day,
as dark as dusk all day,
but I was sick of being stuck indoors
and anyway I like my routine
and I was nearly there,
my yellow bag
bright against the snow,
when I saw it,
a massive cow
hunched against the glass,
it must have skidded on its tiny hooves
and crashed against the solid glass door,
and no one was about,
which was odd,
I peered into the café, I remember,
and saw a swimsuit drying on a hook
and blood,
what looked like blood,
on the tiles,
pools of blood from the wounded cow,
or was I just imagining the cow
the way you do when you're stiff with cold
and think you might have harmed those you love.

THE MAN WITH SNOW-WHITE SKIN

His curly hair a tiny bit too long,
his swimming-trunks a tiny bit too tight,
he waves at me like someone in a dream
waving at me
as they fall past.

A WOMAN WITH A BUNCH OF RED ROSES

Afterwards I walk the six miles home,
gliding through the snow
like a cat
and meeting not a soul all the way
until I reach the florist's where a woman,
balanced on a pair of kitten heels,
a giant bunch of roses in her arms,
almost knocks me over in the gutter
as if to say *why walk when you can totter.*

HAVING FUN WITH BABIES

Because a group of mothers
in the shallow end
are throwing rosy babies around
like little parcels
in a sorting-office
that only sorts the most exciting parcels,
I pity normal people
on dry land
who don't know what they're missing
and don't want to know.

AN OLD MAN BLUE WITH COLD

An old man,
blue with cold,
in pinstriped swimming-trunks,
lowers himself down
into the pool
where icy ripples
wrap around his knees,
I see him flinch
(I flinched from my mother,
her ring,
where is it now, I wonder,
blue),
down he goes,
backwards,
rung by rung,
and nobody's unkind enough to look,
to say, or to appear to be saying,
he should have given up
years ago.

THE WOMAN WITH THE PLAIT

Although the sour-faced woman with the plait
reminds me of my sister,
that's not fair,
my sister was a hundred times more miserable,
a thousand times,
and I was merciless,
my mother spent the whole of my childhood
pleading with me in a voice like honey
Can't you just be friends?
but I couldn't,
I'd kneel by my bed and pray to God
to send me down a wasp
or a hornet
so I could watch her dance around the drawing room
screaming her pretty little head off.

RABBITS

When he drops me off
'in the middle of nowhere',
my lemon-yellow duffle-bag as usual
stuffed with goggles, oranges, the towel
where rows of identical ducks
like identical pilgrims
who know there is something bigger,
if not what,
who walk towards it in enormous boots,
happy to be understanding nothing,
waddle back and forth without a break,
when he drops me off I round the hill
that's always full of rabbits,
rabbits everywhere,
they're on the banks, they're in the lane, they're everywhere,
they've overrun the garden by the shop,
they've colonised the carpark
and the climbing-frame
and soon they'll be inside,
at the reception desk,
demanding that they need the pool for weddings.

FRIDAY NIGHT AT THE SWIMMING-POOL

Because the pool's so empty,
only me,
the silent couple no one knows the name of
and there, in tears, the pot-bellied man
(look away,
even men can cry,
they can and do,
my brother cried once,
teardrops wobbling on his upper lip,
he cried for us,
he cried for his mother,
he cried—
of course, we all do—
for himself)
because the pool's so empty
we can hear
every little heartbreaking sob.

THE MAN IN PURPLE SWIMMING-TRUNKS

If the six-foot man in purple swimming-trunks
who thunders up and down like a lorry
crammed with badly-packed chandeliers
would only sit and rest for a while,
maybe have some water from the cooler,
those of us he scatters
could regroup.

THE PHOTOGRAPH OF MY DOG IN MY DUFFLE-BAG

Why I keep the photo in my duffle-bag
when it makes me sad
I've no idea,
when I feel sadness
like a pelt
brush against the surface of my mind,
ancient,
furtive,
gentle,
like the powder,
my mother's love,
I couldn't bear to touch,
the powder and the flattened powder-puff,
why I keep the photo, I suppose,
is simply to remind me I was loved,
if you can call it love,
that I was shadowed
by a lurcher,
now a lurcher's ghost.

A VERY DARK BLUE

I go the long way round
because it's snowing,
the sky is blue,
a very dark blue,
the colour of my swimsuit,
almost black,
the colour of the sloes on the mountain,
the lonely little mountain where my mother
wished that I had never been born,
I take the long way home because the snow
is whispering *slow down, my friend,
slow down.*

THE SILENT COUPLE NO ONE REALLY KNOWS

The silent couple no one really knows,
who never talk,
not even to each other,
who always smile
(but they look so sad!)
the couple people say,
to cheer them up,
you're nearly there to,
are already there.

THE WOMAN IN THE SALMON-PINK UNDERWEAR

The man who was 'the man who made me cry'
fed me chocolate kittens in his bed,
I cried because I'd never been so happy,
it was in a bedsit in Romania,
I never say a word about the man,
the tiny vanished world
of his tenderness,
but that's what I am thinking to myself
as side by side we crack our chocolate kittens,
the woman in the salmon-pink underwear
I'm still a bit in awe of, and me.

DELICATE QUESTIONS FROM THE YOUNG DOCTOR

He asks me if I think I experience *feelings,*
not thoughts, he's saying, *feelings,*
in my chest,
(he prods me in the chest)
for example
love, he says, I say I don't know,
he asks me if I think I loved my mother
but again I say I don't know
and then I say it's true I rarely cry
and yes, I say, I know I do like swimming
though when I squash my clothes inside the lockers
(and why do lockers have to be so small
with rattly doors
and fiddly little keys)
I feel sadness, yes,
I don't like leaving them,
alone but for a few human hairs,
my clothes, I mean,
still warm from being worn,
I feel sadness,
sorrow,
I don't know,
as if I've got a mouse in my chest
that can't remember what a mouse is for,
that's searching for a god it can believe in,
a feeling in my chest
like at the hospital
in which a heart I know
is slowly beating
while staff adjust and readjust their tubes.

EXPENSIVE SWIMWEAR

Unlike us
in our expensive swimwear
my friend is ill,
seriously ill,
I probably won't see her again,
I swim all afternoon,
I swim to nowhere,
to somewhere where she's not too young to die.

NO MORE POTATOES

The nurses give her nothing but potatoes,
please, she whispers,
no more potatoes,
no more mashed potato, no more soup,
no more sodden bedsocks,
no more frocks,
no more yellow copulating crocodiles
made of rubber on the taxi dash,
no more starry nights and shimmering lakes.